HERON DANCE PRESS & ART STUDIO
179 Rotax Road
N. Ferrisburg, VT 05473
888-304-3766
www.herondance.org

Printed in China.

Heron Dance donates art to dozens of grassroots wilderness protection groups each year. In
addition, *Heron Dance* supports the Northeast Wilderness Trust with financial donations.

ISBN-10: 1-933937-09-2
ISBN-13: 978-1-933937-09-0

Cover image "Solo Serenity" and back cover image "Surya Namaskara"
by Roderick MacIver. Originals and limited-edition prints of selected artwork are available
through our website at www.herondance.org.

Edited by Ann E. O'Shaughnessy
Designed by Terry Fallon; cover design by Luana Life
Cover art and illustrations by Roderick MacIver of *Heron Dance*

For information about special discounts for bulk purchases,
please contact Ingram Publisher Services at 800-961-7698,
or visit www.herondance.biz

PAUSING FOR BEAUTY

THE HERON DANCE

poetry diary

HERON DANCE

contents

I believe real art, in whatever form it takes, is our essence revealed and expressed. And, to me, this act of courageously offering your essence can benefit the world regardless of the reception and can be a powerful act of Love.

Ann E. O'Shaughnessy, editor of Heron Dance

January is named for Janus, the Roman god of doors and gateways.
The original Roman calendar consisted of 10 months (304 days).
The Romans originally considered winter a monthless period.

january

sunday	monday	tuesday	wednesday	thursday	friday	saturday

My heart was my ship, and I was its captain
　　And its rigging was freedom, and love was its keel.
But still from above me the seagulls they thrilled me,
　　I followed with wonder each swoop and each dive;
And I longed to be with them, to dance o'er the waters,
　　For I spurned the base treasures for which other men strive.

Joseph King

I am in need of music that would flow
Over my fretful, feeling fingertips,
Over my bitter-tainted, trembling lips,
With melody, deep, clear, and liquid-slow.

Oh, for the healing swaying, old and low,
Of some song sung to rest the tired dead,
A song to fall like water on my head,
And over quivering limbs, dream flushed to glow.

Elizabeth Bishop, from "Sonnet,"
with thanks to Friends of Silence

Sand sea sky
Elements of truth
Along the shore
Of essential being

Feel the pulse of the earth
A beat so strong and sure
Notice
    Listen
        Touch the core
There is no falseness here

Look at the horizon
Feel the cool breeze
And the warm sun
Find your place
In the gull's cry
In the trinity
Of sand sea sky

Elizabeth M. Cheatham,
Heron Dance *reader*

Last Night as I Was Sleeping

Last night as I was sleeping,
I dreamt—marvelous error!—
that a spring was breaking
out in my heart.
I said: Along which secret aqueduct,
Oh water, are you coming to me,
water of a new life
that I have never drunk?
Last night as I was sleeping,
I dreamt—marvelous error!—
that I had a beehive
here inside my heart.
And the golden bees
were making white combs
and sweet honey
from my old failures.
Last night as I was sleeping,
I dreamt—marvelous error!—
that a fiery sun was giving
light inside my heart.
It was fiery because I felt
warmth as from a hearth,
and sun because it gave light
and brought tears to my eyes.
Last night as I slept,
I dreamt—marvelous error!—
that it was God I had
here inside my heart.

Antonio Machado

Do not stand at my grave and weep
I am not there. I do not sleep.

I am a thousand winds that blow.
I am the diamond glint on snow.
I am the sunlight on ripened grain.
I am the gentle autumn rain.

When you wake in the morning bush
I am the swift, uplifting rush
of quiet birds in circling flight.
I am the soft starlight at night.

Do not stand at my grave and weep.
I am not there. I do not sleep.

Mary E. Frye

9

The great sea stirs me.
The great sea sets me adrift,
it sways me like the weed
on a river-stone.

The sky's height stirs me.
The strong wind blows through my mind.
It carries me with it,
and moves my inner parts with joy.

Uvanuk, woman shaman of the
Ingloolik Inuit, recorded by
Knud Rasmussen in the early 1920s

Summer Night Storm

The ranting of the gods, this tumbling sky,
this wind-strong rain which pelts against my cheek,
the world re-lit by lightning, and the lie
of tall sea grass low bent against the sand.
I stand here, strangely still, with all the world
tumultuous at my feet, and yet my heart
is stronger than the roaring wind that swirls
about my body, taut against its force;
that blows my eyelids shut, that locks my lips,
lest all my spirit end its restlessness
in one wild song.

Jane Tyson Clement

My work as a poet, as an editor, translator, and critic is rooted in my conviction that poetry saved me from a lifetime of misery; poetry helped me find myself as only a lifelong commitment can; devotion to poetry came to mean an authentic search for a moral and disciplined life, a kadō, or "way of poetry," not unlike that to which Saigyō, Bashō, and other Zen poets ascribed. I wanted to make the gift the work of a lifetime. I sought a life of gratitude and revolutionary conviction. My commitment would be to the way of poetry, not to its sycophants or celebrities.

Sam Hamill, from The Gift of Tongues: Twenty-Five Years of Poetry from Copper Canyon Press

February was named for the Roman god Februus, the god of purification.
January and February were the last two months to be added to the Roman calendar,
about 700 BC, in order to bring the calendar in line with a standard lunar year.

february

sunday	monday	tuesday	wednesday	thursday	friday	saturday

Name

You know what
mystery
is beauty
and beauty
to be so close
to the truth,

your truth
which you live so closely.

You don't even know
its rules,
your game.

I am awed
in your presence.
Wind-filled hawk,
the cobbled fish,
on course,
knowing no other.

Given choice
we learn
there is none
to our name.

Coyote is border,
antelope, wind.

And so we must
learn again
who we are.

Lyn Dalebout

From above, to a hawk, the bend must appear only natural and I for the moment inseparably a part, like salmon or a flower. I cannot say well enough how this single perception has dismantled my loneliness.

Barry Lopez

Today I have grown taller from walking
with the trees
The seven sister poplars who go
softly in a line
And I think my heart is white for
its parlay with a star
That trembled out at night and
hung above the pine.

Mary Cooper Back,
written at age 17

To fly we must dance
With our longest shadows in
The brightest sunlight.

Louise Rader

4 a.m. in Katmandu

My wife Laurie and I celebrated our 25th anniversary with a trip to Nepal.
We learned about many things, including jet lag.

It's 4 a.m. in Katmandu
I lie awake in the silent room
I hear my lady stir and rise
she comes and lays close by my side.

I turn and gather her to me
and gently ravish every crease
we feel our love ignite and leap
and give ourselves to grateful heat
and afterwards the birds
the sparrows stir
and the pigeons land
on the corrugated roof
in a mating dance
and then fly off
like fan belts chirping
and the roosters crow
and the dogs are barking
and we're aglow

And we are so full
we are so full
the world is so full
our lives are so full!
My arm across her lovingly
shares the warmth of her body
with the coolness of the morning air
and we're basking in this moment rare

and the kitchens crackle
in the streets below
and the rickshaws rattle
on the cobblestone
and the sun slips down
the undulating wall
and the awareness dawns
that we have it all

Will Danforth, from
Grey Dawn Breaking

at Read's Landing, MN, late February

at noon two dozen bald eagles
more than I had expected
perch high in the black webworks of oaks
searching the bluegray waves for walleyes
or soar and soar.   breasting the gusts
an ashy gray day   abandoned by sunlight
streaked with the sharp flights of mergansers
the exotic iridescence of wood ducks
blessed by a rare sea–duck   a white–winged scoter whose
blackish dark brown body sporting white wing-patches
dives and bobs   dives and bobs
alone thousands of miles from the ocean
and suddenly sailing down
in the center of the wind-torn bay
a golden eagle so dark
brown
lancelike
        feathers of his crown and neck
        washed with gold

Robert Schuler

Storm's End

Sky breaks open
just before dusk
as you stand in a
great wild silence
know that you've
made the right choice:
to weather the storm
and steal this moment
from the gods,
to rejoice
breath-by-breath
fully aware
that just being here
so utterly alive
in the teeth of the world
with a belly full of smiles
is to prevail.

Walt McLaughlin

November 1998

When we picked persimmons
off the tree,
handling each orange globe
as if it were a sun,
leaves around your head
made a golden halo,
sky bluer than blue,
and we knew that soon
wind would scatter leaves,
bare tree'd stand naked
against grey sky,
and this golden ripening time
would leave us too.

Later, when you asked
what made me happy,
and I said "picking persimmons,"
you seemed surprised, and I
had no words to say how
whole and sweet these moments are
before the ripe fruit falls.

Diana Rothman

The one man who should never attempt an explanation of a poem is its author. If the poem can be improved by its author's explanations, it never should have been published, and if the poem cannot be improved by its author's explanations, the explanations are scarcely worth reading.

Archibald MacLeish

In ancient Rome, March was called Martius,
so named after the Roman god of war and
was considered a lucky time to begin a war.

march

sunday	monday	tuesday	wednesday	thursday	friday	saturday

If you could only see your beauty,
     For you are greater than the sun.
Why are you withered and shriveled in this position of dust?
A basketful of bread sits on your head
     But you beg for crusts from door to door.
You are more precious than both heaven and earth.
You know not your own worth.
Sell not yourself at a little price,
     being so precious in the eyes of God.

Rumi

And there is a Catskill eagle in some souls
that can alike dive down
into the blackest gorges,
and soar out of them again
and become invisible
in the sunny places.

Herman Melville

A Wild Grace

   for Bill Mason

Dawn comes first along the spine of the river
Wood smoke and wet ash, mist.
A gull on a grey stone
                    keeping her watch.

Your bags lashed tight—
     fitted against the pale ribs
          the slender body of the canoe—
                    you push off.

Remember Abraham? Remember Sarah? Remember
     the long red thread of their desert journey
          as it passed through weariness
               as it passed through the terror
                    as it passed through love's narrow eye?

          You head out

And what is faithfulness, if not this?
     Climbing up and down the cold white rungs
          the blue ladders of the sea
     A long red canoe rounding a difficult point,
                    an uncertain sky

A wild grace spread out to greet you.

          Cheryl Hellner, reader

You get up in the morning, shake the dew off of your mind,
As the sun pours like honey through the ponderosa pine
You're living every moment as if you've just arrived,
Because you know what it means to be alive.

Jim Stoltz, from "All Along the Great Divide"

Place a twig among
unborn Wrens
and the mother
will feel the need
to destroy the nest
and fly into the ocean
which is not her home.

Rock Wren is not a hard little bird;
she suffers in the cold
and has to winter
in the tumbled slate
on Three Kings Mountain.
She sleeps in fits.
The dream is always the same:

the sun
the cold river.

The crows won't even play
on this turf.
There is big work
in other parts.
And wren has a throat
reserved for cricket
and song.
It is cricket and song
that lead her
under moonlight
over stone.

Rick Smith, from
The Wren Notebook

I think over again
My small adventures
My fears
Those small ones that seemed
so big
For all of the vital things
I had to get and to reach
And yet there is only one
great thing
To live and see the great day
that dawns
And the light that fills the world.

from Inuit poems
recorded by Knud Rasmussen
in the early 1920s

finally pulling into my neighborhood
turning the last corner toward home
three deer dance in the light
thrown over the snow-dusted road

Robert Schuler

A good poem is a contribution to reality. The world is never the same once a good poem has been added to it. A good poem helps to change the shape of the universe, helps to extend everyone's knowledge of himself and the world around him.

Dylan Thomas

April was originally the second month of the Roman calendar and had 29 days.
Julius Caesar's calendar reform in 45 BCE resulted in April
having 30 days and becoming the fourth month.

sunday	monday	tuesday	wednesday	thursday	friday	saturday

Asagumori

On the forest path
The leaves fall. In the withered
Grass the crickets sing
Their last songs. Through dew and dusk
I walk the paths you once walked,
My sleeves wet with memory.

Kenneth Rexroth,
from The Silver Swan

The Path Toward Oneness

I see my life
As a path
Toward Oneness.

Sometimes that path is so narrow
I can barely keep my balance
And sometimes
I lose it.

On one side of that path is fear
Always there, always saying
"Hook into me.
Give yourself to me."
And when I do, I lose myself
Lose my power.

On the other side of that path
Is desire
Always there, always calling
"Give yourself to me."
And when I do, I lose myself
Lose my power.

But when on the path
People show up
With important messages
With help, with a hug.
They seem to me
Messengers from God.

I do not know where this path is going.
In my finer moments
I don't care
I surrender to it
Surrender to Beauty.

Some indigenous peoples believe
That when we die
Our soul continues living
But our ego dies
Our separateness disappears
And we meld
Into the Love Energy.

I like that image.

Roderick MacIver

45

Every stump is sacred.
Every stump a saint.
Every silted river a church to which
the pilgrim salmon return.
Every breath of wind a love song.
We worship the wetlands,
bow to the fern, the rock,
the holy salamander,
the blood of sweet water,
the body of moss.

Gary Lawless

Zion Narrows

Great stone walls shut out stars
to the east and west, loom and close
as night deepens. A breeze
stirs the willows. River.
Dark sandstone seems to breathe.
A thin new moon struggles
over the brooding cliffs
and glitters, askew
in the brimming water. Shadows lurk
in the cottonwoods. A night creature
slides into the clearing,
moves toward the river, seems to bend,
drink. It blends into sighing night,
the haunted canyon,
its warm wind,
crescent moon, shadows,
deep-throated song of water.

David Lee

Love
an ocean
with invisible
shores,
with
no shores.

If you
are wise
you will
not swim
in it.

Rabi'ah bent Ka'b,
Sufi poet

Emergers for the Fuel
Green River, Wyoming

Swallows compete with trout
for caddis flies, yellow sallys,
stoneflies, green leafhoppers.
Ravens hurl their old-woman-cries,
a magpie calls, yellow warblers chirp.
The mayfly deposits her ova on the water.
As the rainbow trout rises to take her:
the silver and splash,
the cloud-burst of color,
sky in water.
Now the nighthawk, then the sun
settles down behind the dam—
one more cloud to set on fire.

Marcyn Clements, 19 July MM

I've decided to make up my mind
about nothing, to assume the water mask,
to finish my life disguised as a creek,
an eddy, joining at night the full,
sweet flow, to absorb the sky,
to swallow the heat and cold, the moon
and the stars, to swallow myself
in ceaseless flow.

Jim Harrison, from "Cabin Poem"

What did you find in the fields today,
you who have wandered so far away?
I found a wind-flower, small and frail,
and a crocus cup like a holy grail;
I found a hill that was clad in gorse,
a new-built nest, and a streamlet's source;
I saw a star and a moonlit tree;
I listened … I think God spoke to me.

Hilda Rostron, with thanks to
Friends of Silence

I don't believe how much time I have to spend listening to even get one poem. It is pathetic. I have to keep going out alone to Yellowstone just to listen. Sometimes nothing will happen, and yet I know that something is happening during that time of listening, but I may not "produce a result." It is a kind of layering. IT is the years and years of years of visiting similar places. I wish I could say what it was. I just know that it is very important.

True poetry is what does not pretend to be poetry. It is in the dogged drafts of a few maniacs seeking the new encounter.

Beth Archer, from The Voice of Things *(edited)*

The month may have been named for the Greek goddess Maia,
who was identified with the Roman goddess of fertility,
Bona Dea, whose festival was held in May.

may

sunday	monday	tuesday	wednesday	thursday	friday	saturday

All that matters is what you love
and what you love is who you are
and who you are is where you are
and where you are is where you will be
when death takes you across the river.

You can't avoid the journey but
you can wake up ... now
and see where you've been
and where you are going.

John Squadra, from This Ecstasy

The bud
stands for all things,
even for those things that don't flower,
for everything flowers, from within, of self-blessing;
though sometimes it is necessary
to reteach a thing its loveliness,
to put a hand on its brow
of the flower
and retell it in words and in touch
it is lovely
until it flowers again from within, of self-blessing

Galway Kinnell,
from "Saint Francis and the Sow"

Close your eyes and you will see clearly
Cease to listen and you will hear truth
Be silent and your heart will sing
Seek no contact and you will find union
Be still and you will move forward in the tide of the spirit
Be gentle and you will not need strength
Be patient and you will achieve all things
Be humble and you remain whole.

Taoist meditation

Sometimes, when a bird cries out,
Or the wind sweeps through a tree,
Or a dog howls in a far-off farm,
I hold still and listen a long time.

My world turns and goes back to the place
Where, a thousand forgotten years ago,
The bird and the blowing wind
Were like me, and were my brothers.

My soul turns into a tree,
And an animal, and a cloud bank.
Then changed and odd it comes home
And asks me questions. What should I reply?

Hermann Hesse

Wild Geese

You do not have to be good.
You do not have to walk on your knees
For a hundred miles through the desert, repenting.
You only have to let the soft animal of your body
love what it loves.
Tell me about your despair, yours, and I will tell you mine.
Meanwhile the world goes on.
Meanwhile the sun and the clear pebbles of the rain
are moving across the landscapes,
over the prairies and the deep trees,
the mountains and the rivers.
Meanwhile the wild geese, high in the clean blue air,
are heading home again.
Whoever you are, no matter how lonely,
the world offers itself to your imagination,
calls to you like the wild geese, harsh and exciting—
over and over announcing your place
in the family of things.

Mary Oliver, from Dream Work

Namaste

I honor the place in you
in which
the entire universe dwells.
I honor the place in you
which is
love, truth, light and peace.
When you are in that place
in you,
and I am in that place
in me,

We are one

James R. Dolan

Eagle Poem

To pray you open your whole self
To sky, to earth, to sun, to moon
To one whole voice that is you.
And know there is more
That you can't see, can't hear
Can't know except in moments
Steadily growing, and in languages
That aren't always sound but other
Circles of motion.
Like eagle that Sunday morning
Over Salt River, circled in blue sky
In wind, swept our hearts clean
With sacred wings.
We see you, see ourselves and know
That we must take the utmost care
And kindness in all things.
Breathe in, knowing we are made of
All this, and breathe, knowing
We are truly blessed because we
Were born, and die soon, within a
True circle of motion,
Like eagle rounding out the morning
Inside us.
We pray that it will be done
In beauty
In beauty.

Joy Harjo

I have always known
That at last I would
Take this road, but yesterday
I did not know that it would be today.

*Narithtra, translated by Kenneth Rexroth,
from* One Hundred Poems
from the Japanese

The greatness of a poem is not that it portrays the thing observed or experienced, but that it portrays the poet's vision cued off by her encounter with the reality.

Rollo May

June is named after the Roman goddess Juno,
wife of Jupiter and equivalent to the
Greek goddess Hera.

june

sunday	monday	tuesday	wednesday	thursday	friday	saturday

I went off with fists in my torn pockets;
My coat was completely threadbare.
I followed you, Muse, where you led me,
Dreamed of loves—ah—so fine and so rare.

Rimbaud, from "Ma Boheme"
from Memoirs *by Pierre Trudeau*

Summer Night

Moonlight and loon wails slip
through the open window
on a fretful breeze drunk
of stargazer lilies
heavy with honey—
lusty fragrance.

William Borden

Inebriate of air am I,
And debauchee of dew.

Emily Dickinson

I wandered lonely as a cloud
That floats on high o'er vales and hills
When all at once I saw a crowd,
A host of golden daffodils;
Beside the lake beneath the trees
Fluttering and dancing in the breeze.

William Wordsworth, from "Daffodils"

I will not die an unlived life.
I will not live in fear
of falling or catching fire.
I choose to inhabit my days,
to allow my living to open me,
to make me less afraid,
more accessible;
to loosen my heart
until it becomes a wing,
a torch, a promise.
I choose to risk my significance,
to live so that which came to me as seed
goes to the next as blossom,
and that which came to me as blossom,
goes on as fruit.

Dawna Markova

If the Earth is a woman
    I have been her lover.

Watching the little fish swim
    in the dark rivers of her heart
    touching the hidden flowers
    of her lips beneath the rough bark
    of cliffs above the sea.

If the Earth is a woman
    I have tasted of her salt
    and of her honey too
    and seen her face beneath
    the moonlit mirrored ice
    before she melted in the liquid
    warmth of spring.

If the Earth is a woman
    we have known each other,
    will know again
    until not even the wind
    can separate our dust.

John Squadra, from This Ecstasy

Come dance with the west wind
and touch all the mountaintops.
Sail o'er the canyons and on to the stars.
And reach for the heavens and
          hope for the future,
and all that we can be, not what we are.

John Denver, from the song,
"The Eagle and the Hawk"

So when you finally step out of the boat
we find everything holds us
and everything confirms our courage.
And if you wanted to drown you could,
but you don't because finally
after all this struggle
and all these years
you don't want to any more.
You simply have had enough of drowning,
and you want to live
and you want to love.

David Whyte, from "True Love"

A poem begins with a lump in the throat, a home-sickness or a love-sickness. It is a reaching-out toward expression; an effort to find fulfillment. A complete poem is one where the emotion has found its thought and the thought has found the words.

Robert Frost

July was renamed for Julius Caesar; previously, it was called Quintilis in Latin, since it was the fifth month in the Roman calendar. Because of its origin, until the 18th century this month's name was pronounced the same way as the name "Julie."

july

sunday	monday	tuesday	wednesday	thursday	friday	saturday

Prayer for the Wild Voice

for Nina

Poetry is the natural prayer of the human soul. —Rilke

1

A long dark curve is the poem in your body
is the river
is the loon's throat.
Have you ever asked yourself how
the loon's voice
opens?

2

You know it first as change in the body.
Even if the blue place you are dreaming
is no longer there
you must begin.
Something that desires to lift
these heavy bones
something simple
and beautiful
miraculous as a feather
forms along the blade
of each wing.

3

Poised, no longer
settled
you wait as every part of you
sheds
what once was,
and is no longer
necessary.
Close to shore you prepare.
And what will it cost you?
And what is this
haunting and wild, now
still in your throat, now
trembling
Set it free
whatever it may cost you
set it free.

Cheryl Hellner, reader

The Question

I wake to darkness
wrapped tightly around ponderosa
pines, tangled in the juniper bark,
collected and held in this small valley
by stout cliffs of sandstone.

Above, a sky is born shiny blue.
Dawn licks the underside of
cottony cumulus pink, while I
walk the dark road, deeper
into the forest to ask why
new dawn follows the night with
only the promise of new darkness.

A black crow flying above the
tops of trees, caws the
clouds white, collecting the
remaining dusk in her feathers—
an old matron collecting wild berries
in her apron. And a new sun
held back now by the most delicate
web of pine needles and dew, begins
to fill the forest, abiding only
the darkness of its own shadow.

The day has fully arrived.
In the distance, a squirrel barks and
a Steller's jay chirps loudly from a treetop
at the new sun, as if pleasantly
surprised to find himself and the world
alive this morning.

I walk the sun mottled road to the
cabin, the moment for questions
now passed.

Bear, from Until the Sleeper Speaks

The Source

Before I die,
I want to trace
The river to its source:
The damp, black earth,
The mountainside,
And smell the leaves and
Needles on the floor,
Be speckled in the
Light and shadows
Of the woods,
And cup my hands,
And catch the wild,
And drink it in.

Paul Clavelle, reader

She who reconciles the ill-matched threads
of her life, and weaves them gratefully
into a single cloth--
it's she who drives the loudmouths from the hall
and clears it for a different celebration

where the one guest is you.
In the softness of evening
it's you she receives.

You are the partner of her loneliness,
the unspeaking center of her monologues.
With each disclosure you encompass more
and she stretches beyond what limits her,
to hold you.

Rainer Maria Rilke, from The Book of
Hours: Love Poems to God

And the end of all our exploring
Will be to arrive where we started
And know the place for the first time

T.S. Eliot

The world is rude, silent, incomprehensible at first,
nature is incomprehensible at first,
Be not discouraged, keep on,
there are divine things well envelop'd,
I swear to you there are divine beings
more beautiful than words can tell.

Walt Whitman

May today there be peace within.

May you trust God that you are exactly where you are meant to be.

May you not forget the infinite possibilities that are born of faith.

May you use those gifts that you have received, and pass on the love that has been given to you.

May you be content knowing you are a child of God.

Let this presence settle into your bones, and allow your soul the freedom to sing, dance, praise and love. It is there for each and every one of us.

Saint Therese of Lisieux

It happens that, as time goes by and I use English more, it grows less alien to me, but I feel the real medium for poets is silence, so I could be writing in any language to reflect the inner silence to give it body. That is all we are doing. We use the voice to make the silence more present. It's like in archi-tecture where the medium is not really stone nor metal but the space they enclose. We use materials—brick, glass, words—to inflect space both outer and inner. So I would say the real medium of poetry is inner space, the silence of our deepest interior.

Li Young Lee, from "The Sun Magazine," *August 2005*

August was named in honor of Caesar Augustus. The month reputedly
has 31 days because Augustus wanted as many days as Julius Caesar's July.
It was originally called Sextilis, the sixth month in the Roman calendar.

august

sunday	monday	tuesday	wednesday	thursday	friday	saturday

Breathless
Mendota Fire Tower trail, atop
Clinch Mountain, Southwest Virginia

As we'd felt the silence
of that long abandoned
summit crackle under
shuffling boots,
huffing
up a final brushy
rise—needled
treetops
parting to blue
realms—two buzzards
leapt
from that stilted
shack
to trail their
great fused
shadow
over us: on that long
bright climb
we'd spied our
limits,
like
a gasp, below flickering
heights of blue.

Dan Stryk

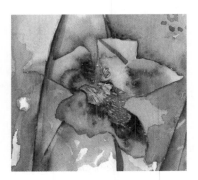

Delight

unexpectedly
coming upon
clusters
of wild
iris
purpling
mountain
morning
streams

Maurice Kenny, reader

In the quiet of this place
in the dark of the night
I wait and watch.

In the stillness of my soul
and from its fathomless depths
the senses of my heart are awake to You.

For fresh soundings of life
for new showings of light
I search for the silence of my spirit,
O Blessing God.

J. Philip Newell,
Celtic Benediction

Cedar Mountain

For some it must be thunder. The mass
of clouds piling over the mountains,
great dark-bellied sky
crackling with ragged light. Deer
rushing through the fragile spaces
we call silence toward a groaning sanctuary
of swaying pine. High meadow
drenched with rain.

For others fragrance. Moist earth
almost forgotten over winter,
a frail scent of budding aspen.
Bubble of willow springs. Bees
hovering delicate pink and white
blossoms spreading an emerging meadow
through rotting snow.

David Lee, from So Quietly the Earth

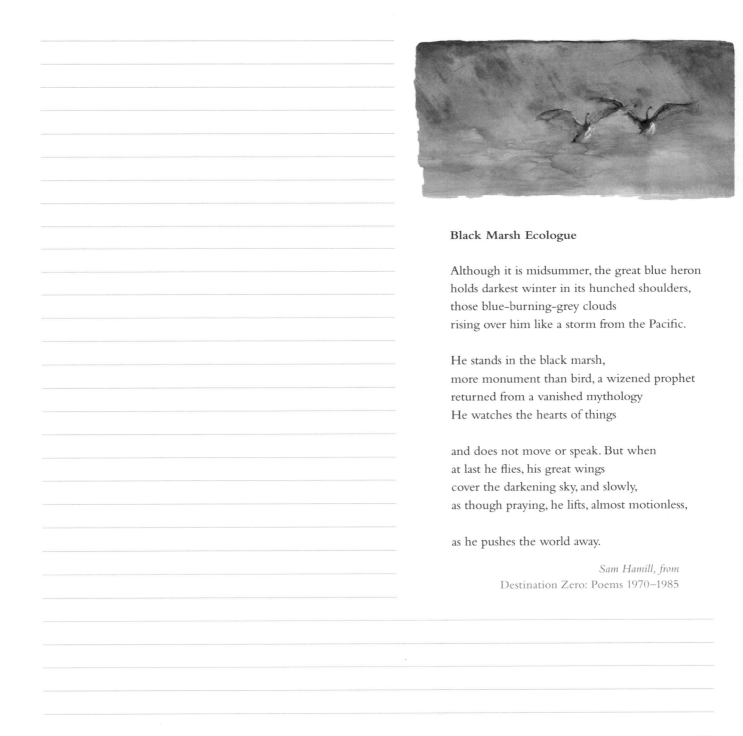

Black Marsh Ecologue

Although it is midsummer, the great blue heron
holds darkest winter in its hunched shoulders,
those blue-burning-grey clouds
rising over him like a storm from the Pacific.

He stands in the black marsh,
more monument than bird, a wizened prophet
returned from a vanished mythology
He watches the hearts of things

and does not move or speak. But when
at last he flies, his great wings
cover the darkening sky, and slowly,
as though praying, he lifts, almost motionless,

as he pushes the world away.

Sam Hamill, from
Destination Zero: Poems 1970–1985

Trees dance
Even on the stillest days.
The dance forms
In the upward arc of the trunk
And explodes
As the canopy catapults
Into the sunlight.

Function cannot
Abide the spontaneity
Of the dance.
The tree is milled,
Its dance buried
Beneath planes and right angles.

I work the milled cube with mallet and gouge
Feeling for the dance.

Sometimes the dance favors the bowl.

Sometimes it is lost.

Kees Wagenvoord

The spotted hawk swoops by and accuses me,
he complains of my gab and loitering.

I too am not a bit tamed, I too am untranslatable,
I sound my barbaric yawp over the roofs of the world.

The last scud of day holds back for me,
It flings my likeness after the rest and true as any on the shadow'd wilds,
It coaxes me to the vapor and the dusk.

I depart as air, I shake my white locks at the runaway sun,
I effuse my flesh in eddies, and drift it in lacy jags.

I bequeath myself to the dirt to grow from the grass I love,
If you want me again look for me under your boot-soles.

You will hardly know who I am or what I mean,
But I shall be good health to you nevertheless,
And filter and fibre your blood.

Failing to fetch me at first keep encouraged,
Missing me one place search another,
I stop somewhere waiting for you.

Walt Whitman, from "Song of Myself,"
found in the new edition of Earth, My Likeness

Athletes take care of their bodies. Writers must similarly take care of the sensibility that houses the possibility of poems. There is nourishment in books, other art, history, philosophies—in holiness and in mirth. It is in honest hands-on labor also; I don't mean to indicate a preference for the scholarly life. And it is in the green world—among people, and animals, and trees for that matter, if one genuinely cares about trees. A mind that is lively and inquiring, compassionate, curious, angry, full of music, full of feeling, is a mind full of possible poetry. Poetry is a life-cherishing force. And it requires a vision—a faith, to use an old-fashioned term. Yes, indeed. For poems are not words, after all, but fires for the cold, ropes let down to the lost, something as necessary as bread in the pockets of the hungry. Yes, indeed.

Mary Oliver

The name September comes from the Latin word *septem*, for "seven."
September was the seventh month of the Roman calendar until 153 BC.

september

sunday	monday	tuesday	wednesday	thursday	friday	saturday

If you listen,
not to the pages or preachers
but to the smallest flower
growing from a crack
in your heart,
you will hear a great song
moving across a wide ocean
whose water is the music
connecting all the islands
of the universe together,
and touching all
you will feel it
touching you
around you …
embracing you
with light.

John Squadra, from
This Ecstasy

I know that I am one with beauty
And that my comrades are one.
Let our souls be mountains,
Let our spirits be stars,
Let our hearts be worlds.

Gaelic Mantra

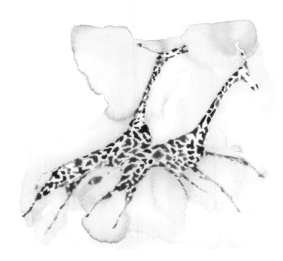

Divine am I inside and out, and I make holy whatever I touch or am touch'd from,
The scent of these arm-pits aroma finer than prayer....

If I worship one thing more than another, it shall be the spread of my own body....

I dote on myself ... there is that lot of me and all so luscious,
Each moment and whatever happens thrills me with joy.

Walt Whitman, from "Song of Myself"

Grace has been defined as the
outward expression of the inward
harmony of the soul.

William Hazlitt

For All

Ah to be alive
      on a mid–September morn
      fording a stream
      barefoot, pants rolled up
      holding boots, pack on,
      sunshine, ice in the shadows,
      northern rockies.

Rustle and shimmer of icy creek waters
stones turn underfoot, small and hard on toes
      cold nose dripping
      singing inside
      creek music, heart music
      smell of sun on gravel.

      I pledge allegiance.

I pledge allegiance to the soil
      of Turtle Island
      one ecosystem
      in diversity
      under the sun—
With joyful interpenetration for all.

Gary Snyder, from Axe Handles

eagles in the rain

young eagles circling over the river
winding round the pines
in the rain   I did not think
they would come out into it
but they have   and now they dive
down   shooting through the ravines

Robert Schuler

The breeze at dawn has secrets to tell you.
Don't go back to sleep.

You must ask for what you really want.
Don't go back to sleep.

People are going back and forth across the doorsill
where the two worlds touch.

The door is round and open.
Don't go back to sleep.

Rumi, translated by Coleman Barks

Poetry should be like fireworks, packed carefully and
artfully, ready to explode with unpredictable effects.

Lilian Moore

October is from the Latin word *octo* for "eight." It was the eighth month in the Roman calendar until a monthless winter period (summer in the southern hemisphere) was divided between January and February.

october

sunday	monday	tuesday	wednesday	thursday	friday	saturday

The Lake Isle of Innisfree

I will arise and go now, and go to Innisfree
And a small cabin build there, of clay and wattles made
Nine bean rows will I have there, a hive for the honeybee
And live alone in the bee-loud glade.

And I shall have some peace there, for peace
Comes dropping slow.
Dropping from the veils of the morning to where the
cricket sings;
There midnight's all a glimmer, and noon a purple glow,
And evening full of the Linnet's wings.

I will arise and go now, for always night and day
I hear lake water lapping with low sounds by shore;
While I stand on the roadway, or on the pavements grey,
I hear it in the deep heart's core.

W.B. Yeats

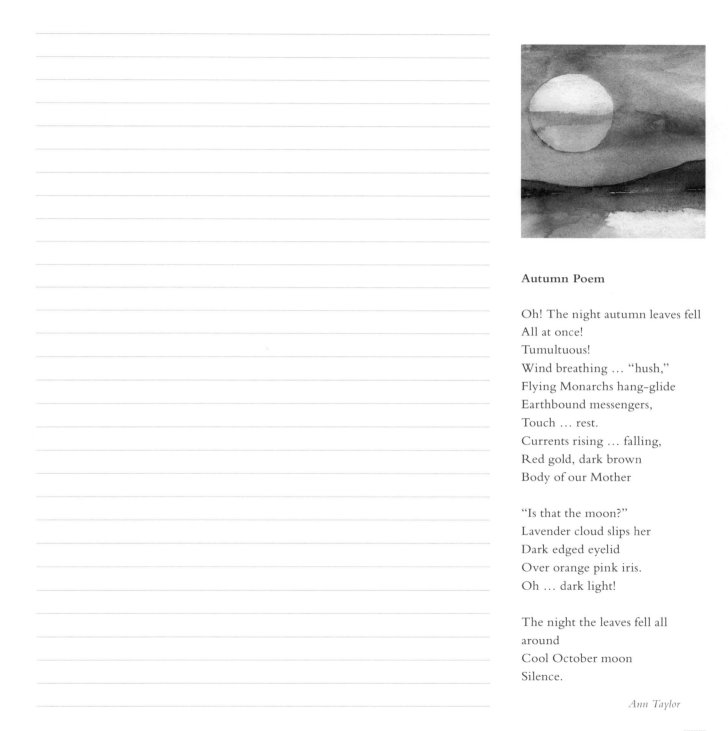

Autumn Poem

Oh! The night autumn leaves fell
All at once!
Tumultuous!
Wind breathing ... "hush,"
Flying Monarchs hang-glide
Earthbound messengers,
Touch ... rest.
Currents rising ... falling,
Red gold, dark brown
Body of our Mother

"Is that the moon?"
Lavender cloud slips her
Dark edged eyelid
Over orange pink iris.
Oh ... dark light!

The night the leaves fell all
around
Cool October moon
Silence.

Ann Taylor

Green Mountain Gavotte

Cavort with me
on a boulder
midstream
while the leaves
rot and eddy
and madwater
din is drowned
by the spume of hearts.

Lisa Beatman

there
on that high ledge
small body against the sky
a bird stands on its bird legs
slight threads of grounding

tiny those legs
walking the earth

huge the sky
holding its flight

what part earth?
what part sky?

Elizabeth M. Cheatham

Brimming Water

Under my feet the moon
Glides along the river.
Near midnight, a gusty lantern
Shines in the heart of night.
Along the sandbars flocks
Of white egrets roost.
Each one clenched like a fist.
In the wake of my barge
The fish leap, cut the water,
And dive and splash.

Tu Fu, translated by Kenneth
Rexroth, from One Hundred
Poems from the Chinese

Who walks with beauty has no need of fear;
The sun and moon and stars keep pace with him;
Invisible hands restore the ruined year,
And time, itself, grows beautifully dim.

David Morton

The Fall

I love the light of autumn:
the fall from grace
through space and into place,
a season between extremes
when we forgive each other and ourselves
for all we have done and not done,
and prepare together
for the darkness and cold to come.

William Clipman

If The Owl Calls Again

at dusk
from the island in the river,
and it's not too cold,

I'll wait for the moon
to rise,
then take wing and glide
to meet him.

We will not speak,
but hooded against the frost
soar above
the alder flats, searching
with tawny eyes.

And then we'll sit
in the shadowy spruce
and pick the bones
of careless mice,

while the long moon drifts
toward Asia
and the river mutters
in its icy bed.

And when the morning climbs
the limbs
we'll part without a sound,

fulfilled, floating
homeward as
the cold world awakens.

John Haines. from The Owl in
the Mask of the Dreamer

He who clings to his work
will create nothing that endures.

The Master does his job
and then stops.
He understands that the universe
is forever out of control,
and that trying to dominate events
goes against the current of the Tao.

Because he believes in himself,
he doesn't try to convince another.
Because he is content with himself,
he doesn't need others' approval.
Because he accepts himself,
the whole world accepts him.

Do your work, then step back.
The only path to serenity.

Knowing others is intelligence;
knowing yourself is true wisdom.
Mastering others is strength;
mastering yourself is true power.

I have just three things to teach:
simplicity, patience, compassion.

Excerpts from the Tao Te Ching,
translation by Stephen Mitchell

My work is communication that resembles the process of birthing a child, children. Volcanic bursting with word, image, form, and formlessness. Blood and water. From soul, via heart, to pen, to mouth. Like digging deeply in mud. The scent of life renewed daily. Reinventing the wheel over and over and over again. No excuses for the work with words. Only sheer joy at its very necessity.

Poetry is created because we are lonely, scared, grateful, joyous, decaying, grieving, angry, visionary, vital. To make sense of life. Our realities. Both harsh and stunning.

I write because I want to belong and because I do not want to belong. Community calls. The Tribe who knows how to fashion with words. Who cares about the meaning of life, who desires frivolity and fierceness. Who knows that like fresh, clean water, poetry exalts life, and saves lives, and honors all that we know and do not know.

Margot Van Sluytman

November is from the Latin *novem* for "nine," the ninth month in the Roman calendar. The Anglo-Saxons referred to November as the "wind month." November begins on the same day of the week as March every year.

november

sunday	monday	tuesday	wednesday	thursday	friday	saturday

There is stillness
    which captures imagination
    in the gauzy glow of winter fog
      at night.

A peace seen
    in the still branches of pine trees
    tracing the edges of darkness

...brooding secrets
    veiled in mauve mist
    descend to touch earthly planes,

leaving mortal hearts
    beating more quietly,
    leaning forward

...stretching to hear

    the coming storm
    it announces.

Charlaine Coleman

Nowhere and never
And now and forever
I look for a thing
That is looking for me.

Sydney Carter

The Idea of Balance Is To Be Found in Herons and Loons

I just heard a loon-call on a TV ad
and my body gave itself
a quite voluntary shudder,
as in the night in East Africa
I heard the immense barking cough
of a lion, so foreign and indifferent.

But the lion drifts away
and the loon stays close
calling, as she did in my childhood,
in the cold rain a song
that tells the world of men
to keep its distance.

It isn't the signal of another life
or the reminder of anything
except her call: still,
at this quiet point past midnight
the rain is the same rain
that fell so long ago, and the loon
says I'm seven years old again.

At the far ends of the lake
where no one lives or visits—
there are no roads to get there;
you take the watercourse way,
the quiet drip and drizzle
of oars, slight squeak of oarlock,
the bare feet can feel the cold water
move beneath the old wood boat.

At one end the lordly great blue herons
nest at the top of the white pine;
at the other end the loons,
just after daylight in cream-colored mist,
drifting with wails that begin as querulous,
rising then into the spheres in volume,
with lost or doomed angels imprisoned
within their breasts.

Jim Harrison, from The Shape of the Journey

This is what I learned: that everybody is talented, original, and has something important to say. Everybody is talented because everybody who is human has something to express. Everybody is original, if she tells the truth, if she speaks from herself. But it must be from her true self and not the self she thinks she should be. So remember these two things: you are talented and you are original. Be sure of that. I say this because self-trust is one of the very most important things in writing....

Brenda Ueland, from If You Want to Write

For The Anniversary of My Death

Every year without knowing it I have passed the day
When the last fires will wave to me
And the silence will set out
Tireless traveller
Like the beam of a lightless star

Then I will no longer
Find myself in life as in a strange garment
Surprised at the earth
And the love of one woman
And the shamelessness of men
As today writing after three days of rain
Hearing the wren sing and the falling cease
And bowing not knowing to what

W.S. Merwin

You enter the forest
at the darkest point,
where there is no path.

Where there is a way or path,
it is someone else's path.

You are not on your own path.

If you follow someone else's way,
you are not going to realize
your potential.

It takes courage
to do what you want.
Other people
have a lot of plans for you.

Nobody wants you to do
what you want to do.

They want you to go on their trip....

Joseph Campbell

In the great night my heart will go out
Toward me the darkness comes rattling
In the great night my heart will go out.

Papago song

Love After Love

The time will come
when, with elation
you will greet yourself arriving
at your own door, in your own mirror
and each will smile at the other's welcome,

and say, sit here. Eat.
You will love again the stranger who was your self.
Give wine. Give bread. Give back your heart
to itself, to the stranger who has loved you

all your life, whom you ignored
for another, who knows you by heart.
Take down the love letters from the bookshelf,

the photographs, the desperate notes,
peel your own image from the mirror.
Sit. Feast on your life.

Derek Walcott

The difference between the right and the nearly right word
is the same as that between lightning and the lightning bug.

Mark Twain

December is from the Latin *decem* for "ten," the tenth month of the Roman calendar. The Anglo-Saxons called it "winter month" or "yule month" because of the custom of burning the yule log around this time of year.

december

sunday	monday	tuesday	wednesday	thursday	friday	saturday

Night in the House by the River

It is late in the year;
Yin and Yang struggle
In the brief sunlight.
On the desert mountains
Frost and snow
Gleam in the freezing night.
Past midnight,
Drums and bugles ring out,
Violent, cutting the heart.
Over the Triple Gorge the Milky Way
Pulsates between the stars.
The bitter cries of thousands of households
Can be heard above the noise of battle.
Everywhere the workers sing wild songs.
The great heroes and generals of old time
Are yellow dust forever now.
Such are the affairs of men
Poetry and letters
Persist in silence and solitude.

Tu Fu, translated by Kenneth Rexroth, from
One Hundred Poems from The Chinese

I met in a wood
a dream pale owl
with eyes that were not blue

and like myself, he was not wise
and he was not good,
but sometimes he was true.

John Squadra,
from This Ecstasy

The soul, like the moon,
is new, and always new again.

And I have seen the ocean
continuously creating.

Since I scoured my mind
and my body, I too, Lalla,
am new, each moment new.

My teacher told me one thing,
Live in the soul.

When that was so,
I began to go naked,
And dance.

Lalla

There is no sense in going further—it's the edge of cultivation,
So they said, and I believed it—broke my land and sowed my crop—
Built my barns and strung my fences in the little border station
Tucked away below the foothills where the trails run out and stop;

Till a voice as bad as Conscience, ran interminable charges
On one everlasting Whisper day and night repeated—so;
"Something hidden. Go and find it. Go and look behind the Ranges—
"Something lost behind the Ranges. Lost and waiting for you. Go!"

Rudyard Kipling, from "The Explorer"

I have been one who loved the wilderness
    Swaggered and softly crept between the mountain peaks
I listened along to the sea's brave music;
    I sang my songs above the shriek of desert winds.

Everett Ruess

Escape

When we get out of the glass bottles of our ego,
and when we escape like squirrels turning in the cages of our personality
and get into the forests again,
we shall shiver with cold and fright,
but things will happen to us
so that we don't know ourselves.

Cool, undying life will rush in,
and passion will make our bodies taut with power,
we shall stamp our feet with new power
and old things will fall down,
we shall laugh, and institutions will curl up like burnt paper.

D. H. Lawrence

Hawks

Surely, you too have longed for this—
to pour yourself out
on the rising circles of the air,
to ride, unthinking,
on the flesh of emptiness.

Can you claim, in your civilized life,
that you have never leaned toward
the headlong dive, the snap of bones,
the chance to be so terrible,
so free from evil, beyond choice?

The air that they are riding
is the same breath as your own.
How could you not remember?
That same swift stillness binds
your cells in balance, rushes
through the pulsing circles of your blood.

Each breath proclaims it—
the flash of feathers, the chance to rest
on such a muscled quietness,
to be in that fierce presence,
wholly wind, wholly wild.

Lynn Ungar

HERON DANCE
Press & Art Studio

A big thank you to all who have supported our efforts to publish work that celebrates the gift of life, the beauty of the natural world, and the goodness of which humans are capable.

Heron Dance Press & Art Studio explores diverse perspectives on the human search for meaning, creativity, and the human connection to the natural world. In addition to wilderness classics, books of inspiration, daybooks, address books, and blank journals, we also sell original artwork, limited-edition prints, and notecards. We publish our quarterly journal, *Heron Dance*, four times a year and offer a free weekly email, *A Pause for Beauty*.

Roderick MacIver, Founder and Artist
Roderick MacIver founded *Heron Dance* in 1995 to celebrate the seeker's journey and the spirit and beauty of all that is wild. Born in Canada, Rod currently splits his time between Vermont and his studio in New York's Adirondacks. His work is inspired by a love of wild nature. Readers and art patrons write hundreds of letters a year to *Heron Dance* responding to the sense of peace and serenity embodied in his watercolors.

Ann O'Shaughnessy, Editor and Writer
Ann O'Shaughnessy joined *Heron Dance* in 2000, bringing with her a love of words and wild nature and a passion for the *Heron Dance* mision: to provide "art, words, and good company for the seeker's journey." She leads Open Heart ~ Wild Soul workshops—an exploration of efforts to live our truth, as well as writing a monthly email, *"Letters from an Open Heart."*

If you would like to learn more or have any questions about other Heron Dance *publications or our artwork, please visit us on the web at www.herondance.org or call us at 888-304-3766.*

2006

january
S	M	T	W	T	F	S
1	2	3	4	5	6	7
8	9	10	11	12	13	14
15	16	17	18	19	20	21
22	23	24	25	26	27	28
29	30	31				

february
S	M	T	W	T	F	S
			1	2	3	4
5	6	7	8	9	10	11
12	13	14	15	16	17	18
19	20	21	22	23	24	25
26	27	28				

march
S	M	T	W	T	F	S
			1	2	3	4
5	6	7	8	9	10	11
12	13	14	15	16	17	18
19	20	21	22	23	24	25
26	27	28	29	30	31	

april
S	M	T	W	T	F	S
						1
2	3	4	5	6	7	8
9	10	11	12	13	14	15
16	17	18	19	20	21	22
$^{23}/_{30}$	24	25	26	27	28	29

may
S	M	T	W	T	F	S
	1	2	3	4	5	6
7	8	9	10	11	12	13
14	15	16	17	18	19	20
21	22	23	24	25	26	27
28	29	30	31			

june
S	M	T	W	T	F	S
				1	2	3
4	5	6	7	8	9	10
11	12	13	14	15	16	17
18	19	20	21	22	23	24
25	26	27	28	29	30	

july
S	M	T	W	T	F	S
						1
2	3	4	5	6	7	8
9	10	11	12	13	14	15
16	17	18	19	20	21	22
$^{23}/_{30}$	$^{24}/_{31}$	25	26	27	28	29

august
S	M	T	W	T	F	S
		1	2	3	4	5
6	7	8	9	10	11	12
13	14	15	16	17	18	19
20	21	22	23	24	25	26
27	28	29	30	31		

september
S	M	T	W	T	F	S
					1	2
3	4	5	6	7	8	9
10	11	12	13	14	15	16
17	18	19	20	21	22	23
24	25	26	27	28	29	30

october
S	M	T	W	T	F	S
1	2	3	4	5	6	7
8	9	10	11	12	13	14
15	16	17	18	19	20	21
22	23	24	25	26	27	28
29	30	31				

november
S	M	T	W	T	F	S
			1	2	3	4
5	6	7	8	9	10	11
12	13	14	15	16	17	18
19	20	21	22	23	24	25
26	27	28	29	30		

december
S	M	T	W	T	F	S
					1	2
3	4	5	6	7	8	9
10	11	12	13	14	15	16
17	18	19	20	21	22	23
$^{24}/_{31}$	25	26	27	28	29	30

2007

january
S	M	T	W	T	F	S
	1	2	3	4	5	6
7	8	9	10	11	12	13
14	15	16	17	18	19	20
21	22	23	24	25	26	27
28	29	30	31			

february
S	M	T	W	T	F	S
				1	2	3
4	5	6	7	8	9	10
11	12	13	14	15	16	17
18	19	20	21	22	23	24
25	26	27	28			

march
S	M	T	W	T	F	S
				1	2	3
4	5	6	7	8	9	10
11	12	13	14	15	16	17
18	19	20	21	22	23	24
25	26	27	28	29	30	31

april
S	M	T	W	T	F	S
1	2	3	4	5	6	7
8	9	10	11	12	13	14
15	16	17	18	19	20	21
22	23	24	25	26	27	28
29	30					

may
S	M	T	W	T	F	S
		1	2	3	4	5
6	7	8	9	10	11	12
13	14	15	16	17	18	19
20	21	22	23	24	25	26
27	28	29	30	31		

june
S	M	T	W	T	F	S
					1	2
3	4	5	6	7	8	9
10	11	12	13	14	15	16
17	18	19	20	21	22	23
24	25	26	27	28	29	30

july
S	M	T	W	T	F	S
1	2	3	4	5	6	7
8	9	10	11	12	13	14
15	16	17	18	19	20	21
22	23	24	25	26	27	28
29	30	31				

august
S	M	T	W	T	F	S
			1	2	3	4
5	6	7	8	9	10	11
12	13	14	15	16	17	18
19	20	21	22	23	24	25
26	27	28	29	30	31	

september
S	M	T	W	T	F	S
						1
2	3	4	5	6	7	8
9	10	11	12	13	14	15
16	17	18	19	20	21	22
$^{23}/_{30}$	24	25	26	27	28	29

october
S	M	T	W	T	F	S
	1	2	3	4	5	6
7	8	9	10	11	12	13
14	15	16	17	18	19	20
21	22	23	24	25	26	27
28	29	30	31			

november
S	M	T	W	T	F	S
				1	2	3
4	5	6	7	8	9	10
11	12	13	14	15	16	17
18	19	20	21	22	23	24
25	26	27	28	29	30	

december
S	M	T	W	T	F	S
						1
2	3	4	5	6	7	8
9	10	11	12	13	14	15
16	17	18	19	20	21	22
$^{23}/_{30}$	$^{24}/_{31}$	25	26	27	28	29

2008

january
S	M	T	W	T	F	S
		1	2	3	4	5
6	7	8	9	10	11	12
13	14	15	16	17	18	19
20	21	22	23	24	25	26
27	28	29	30	31		

february
S	M	T	W	T	F	S
					1	2
3	4	5	6	7	8	9
10	11	12	13	14	15	16
17	18	19	20	21	22	23
24	25	26	27	28	29	

march
S	M	T	W	T	F	S
						1
2	3	4	5	6	7	8
9	10	11	12	13	14	15
16	17	18	19	20	21	22
$^{23}/_{30}$	$^{24}/_{31}$	25	26	27	28	29

april
S	M	T	W	T	F	S
		1	2	3	4	5
6	7	8	9	10	11	12
13	14	15	16	17	18	19
20	21	22	23	24	25	26
27	28	29	30			

may
S	M	T	W	T	F	S
				1	2	3
4	5	6	7	8	9	10
11	12	13	14	15	16	17
18	19	20	21	22	23	24
25	26	27	28	29	30	31

june
S	M	T	W	T	F	S
1	2	3	4	5	6	7
8	9	10	11	12	13	14
15	16	17	18	19	20	21
22	23	24	25	26	27	28
29	30					

july
S	M	T	W	T	F	S
		1	2	3	4	5
6	7	8	9	10	11	12
13	14	15	16	17	18	19
20	21	22	23	24	25	26
27	28	29	30	31		

august
S	M	T	W	T	F	S
					1	2
3	4	5	6	7	8	9
10	11	12	13	14	15	16
17	18	19	20	21	22	23
$^{24}/_{31}$	25	26	27	28	29	30

september
S	M	T	W	T	F	S
	1	2	3	4	5	6
7	8	9	10	11	12	13
14	15	16	17	18	19	20
21	22	23	24	25	26	27
28	29	30				

october
S	M	T	W	T	F	S
			1	2	3	4
5	6	7	8	9	10	11
12	13	14	15	16	17	18
19	20	21	22	23	24	25
26	27	28	29	30	31	

november
S	M	T	W	T	F	S
						1
2	3	4	5	6	7	8
9	10	11	12	13	14	15
16	17	18	19	20	21	22
$^{23}/_{30}$	24	25	26	27	28	29

december
S	M	T	W	T	F	S
	1	2	3	4	5	6
7	8	9	10	11	12	13
14	15	16	17	18	19	20
21	22	23	24	25	26	27
28	29	30	31			

references

"A Wild Grace" by Cheryl Hellner. © 2005 Cheryl Hellner. All rights reserved.

All that matters is what you love by John Squadra. © 1996 John Squadra. All rights reserved. *This Ecstasy*. North Ferrisburg, VT: Heron Dance Press, 2006.

"Asagumori" by Kenneth Rexroth. © 1976 Kenneth Rexroth. All rights reserved. *The Silver Swan*. Port Townsend, WA: Copper Canyon Press, 1976.

"at Read's Landing, MN, late February" by Robert Schuler. © Robert Schuler. All rights reserved.

"Black Marsh Ecologue" by Sam Hamill. © 1995 Sam Hamill. All rights reserved. Reprinted here by permission of Sam Hamill. *Destination Zero: Poems 1970–1985*. Fredonia, NY: White Pine Press, 1995.

"Brimming Water" by Tu Fu, trans. by Kenneth Rexroth. © 1971 Kenneth Rexroth. All rights reserved. *One Hundred Poems from the Chinese*. New York: New Directions Publishing, 1971.

"Night in the House by the River" by Tu Fu, trans. by Kenneth Rexroth. © 1971 Kenneth Rexroth. All rights reserved. *One Hundred Poems from the Chinese*. New York: New Directions Publishing, 1971.

"Cabin Poem" by Jim Harrison. © 2000 Jim Harrrison. All rights reserved. *The Shape of the Journey: New & Collected Poems*. Port Townsend, WA: Copper Canyon Press, 2000.

"Cedar Mountain" by David Lee. © 2002 David Lee. All rights reserved. *So Quietly the Earth*. Port Townsend, WA: Copper Canyon Press, 2004.

"Delight" by Maurice Kenny. © 2006 Maurice Kenny. All rights reserved.

"Eagle Poem" by Joy Harjo. © 1990 Joy Harjo. All rights reserved. *In Mad Love and War*. Middletown, CT: Wesleyan University Press, 1990.

"eagles in the rain" by Robert Schuler. © Robert Schuler. All rights reserved.

"The Fall" by William Clipman. © William Clipman. All rights reserved.

finally pulling into my neighborhood by Robert Schuler. © Robert Schuler. All rights reserved.

"For All" by Gary Snyder. © 2005 Shoemaker & Hoard Publishers. All rights reserved. Reprinted by permission of Shoemaker & Hoard Publishers. *Axe Handles*, reprint edition. Emeryville, CA: Shoemaker & Hoard Publishers; 2005.

I will not die an unlived life by Dawna Markova. © 2000 Dawna Markova. All rights reserved. *I Will Not Die an Unlived Life: Reclaiming Purpose and Passion*. Berkeley, CA: Conari Press, 2000.

I met in a wood by John Squadra. © 1996 John Squadra. All rights reserved. *This Ecstasy*. North Ferrisburg, VT: Heron Dance Press, 2006.

If the Earth is a woman by John Squadra. © 1996 John Squadra. All rights reserved. *This Ecstasy*. North Ferrisburg, VT: Heron Dance Press, 2006.

"If The Owl Calls Again" by John Haines. © 1993 Graywolf Press. All rights reserved. *The Owl in the Mask of the Dreamer: Collected Poems*. Saint Paul, MN: Graywolf Press, 1993. Reprinted by permission of Graywolf Press.

If you listen by John Squadra. © 1996 John Squadra. All rights reserved. *This Ecstasy*. North Ferrisburg, VT: Heron Dance Press, 2006.

"Last Night as I Was Sleeping" by Antonio Machado, trans. by Robert Bly. © 1983 Robert Bly. All rights reserved. Used with permission. *Times Alone: Selected Poems of Antonio Machado*. Middletown, CT: Wesleyan University Press, 1983.

"Love After Love" by Derek Walcott. © 1987 Derek Walcott. All rights reserved. *Collected Poems: 1948–1984*. New York: Ferrar, Strauss & Giroux, 1987.

"Made of Water" by Tom Wisner. © 1997, 1979 Tom Wisner. All right reserved. *Made of Water*, audio recording, 2001.

"Name" by Lyn Dalebout. © 1999 Lyn Dalebout. All rights reserved.

"November 1998" by Diana Rothman. © 1998 Diana Rothman. All rights reserved.

"Prayer for the Wild Voice" by Cheryl Hellner. © 2005 Cheryl Hellner. All rights reserved.

"Saint Francis and the Sow" from *Mortal Acts, Mortal Words* by Galway Kinnell. © 1980 Galway Kinnell. Reprinted by permission of Houghton Mifflin Co. All rights reserved.

"Storm's End" by Walt McLaughlin. © 2002 Walt McLaughlin. All rights reserved.

"Summer Night Storm" by Jane Tyson Clement. © 2000 Bruderhof Foundation. *No One Can Stem the Tide*. www.plough.com: Plough Publishing House, 2000.

To fly we must dance by Louise Rader. © 2005 Louise Rader. All rights reserved.

There is stillness by Charlaine Coleman. © 2005 Charlaine Coleman. All rights reserved.

"When I Die" by Doug Wilson. © 2000 Doug Wilson. All rights reserved.

"Wild Geese" by Mary Oliver, American poet, Pulitzer Prize recipient. © 1986 Mary Oliver. All rights reserved. *Dream Work*. New York: Atlantic Monthly Press, 1986.

"Zion Narrows" by David Lee. © 2002 David Lee. All rights reserved. *So Quietly the Earth*. Port Townsend, WA: Copper Canyon Press, 2004.

list of illustrations

ALSO FROM HERON DANCE PRESS
All titles feature Roderick MacIver watercolors

Heron Dance Book of Love and Gratitude

Heron Dance Press celebrates the open heart and the beauty and mystery that surround us with this book of poetry, book, and interview excerpts. Forty-eight watercolors by Roderick MacIver and selections from the written works of Helen Keller, Dostoevsky, and Henry Miller, among many others. 80 pages.

#1602   *Heron Dance Book of Love and Gratitude* – $12.00

This Ecstasy

This courageous and beautiful book by John Squadra of poems explores, with simplicity, the truths of love and a spiritual life. Some poems are erotic. Some poems expose the truths of life we all share. 91 pages.

#6087   *This Ecstasy* – $10.95

Earth, My Likeness
Nature Poetry of Walt Whitman

A carefully selected collection of poems alongside Roderick MacIver's watercolor art creates a grand tribute. Edited by Howard Nelson. 144 pages.

#6088   *Earth My Likeness* – $11.95

A Natural Wisdom
Gleanings from the Journals of Henry David Thoreau

Walt McLaughlin selects 80 entries from Thoreau's journals that are thought-provoking and insightful. 62 pages.

#6019   *A Natural Wisdom* – $10.00

Forest Under My Fingernails
Reflections and Encounters on Vermont's Long Trail

Years ago we excerpted this book about Walt McLaughlin's wilderness trek. The book sold out but recently has been reprinted. His reflections and encounters are beautifully told. We highly recommend it. 192 pages.

#6085   *Forest Under My Fingernails* – $15.95

True North
with an introduction by Lawrence Millman

In 1929, at the age of 24, Elliott Merrick left his position as an advertising executive in New Jersey and headed up to Labrador to work as an unpaid volunteer for the Grenfell Mission. In 1933 he

wrote True North about his experiences in the northern wilderness, living and working with trappers, Indians and with the nurse he met and married in a remote community. The book describes the hard work and severe conditions, along with the joy and friendship he and his wife experienced. 320 pages

#6086   *True North* – $19.95

Sleeping Island
A Journey to the Edge of the Barrens

In Sleeping Island, Prentice G. Downes records a journey made in 1939 of a North that was soon to be no more, a landscape and a people barely touched by the white man. His respect for the Native Indians and the Inuit, their ways of life, and his love of their land shine through this richly descriptive work. With the kind permission of the Downes family, Heron Dance has republished this book. 288 pages.

#6083   *Sleeping Island* – $19.95